Math Jokes Gift Book

by Ralph Lane

ISBN: 979-8-9857511-9-2

Ralph's gift books make great presents for birthdays, holidays, teacher appreciation, gift baskets, stocking stuffers, bathroom books, vacation books or just for the fun of it. Please consider leaving a review for this book on amazon.com or goodreads.com. You'll also want to read these other fine Ralph Lane books:

Dad Jokes Gift Book
Dad Jokes Halloween Gift Book
Dad Jokes Christmas Gift Book
Dad Jokes Valentine's Day Gift Book
Dad Jokes St. Patrick's Day Gift Book
Dad Jokes Easter Gift Book
Mother's Day Gift Book
Dad Jokes Birthday Gift Book

Table of Contents

Fractionally Funny

There's a fine line between a numerator and a denominator...

Only a fraction of people will get this.

I'm sorry if that last fraction joke turned out to be improper.

Which British monarch loved fractions?

Henry the 1/8

What do you get if you add 31/34 of an apple to 47/53 of an apple?

apple sauce

1/5 of people need to calm down.

They're two-tenths.

How do you know that the fractions x/c, y/c and z/c are on another continent?

Because they're all over c's.

What does a football game have in common with a dollar?

They both have four quarters.

Why was the fraction worried about marrying the decimal?

Because she would have to convert.

Optimist: The glass is half full.

Pessimist: The glass is half empty.

Engineer: The glass is double the necessary size.

Two vegetarian parallel lines...

...never meat.

Math Teacher

Where do math teachers celebrate New Year's Eve?

Times Squared

My math teacher told me I'm average.

That was a 'mean' thing to say.

Did you hear about the fight between the English teacher and the math teacher?

The English teacher said that a double negative is bad while the math teacher said it's a positive.

Why are math teachers such good drummers?

Because they've got such great algo-rhythm.

What did the math teacher say to her misbehaving students?

If I've told you n times, I've told you n+1 times…

Which season do math teachers like the most?

SUMmer

Surprisingly, my math teacher doesn't like numbers. She says that every other one is odd.

I once knew a math teacher who was afraid of negative numbers. He would stop at nothing to avoid them.

Why are math teachers considered to be codependent?

Because they rely on others to solve their problems.

What is a math teacher's favorite type of tree?

geometry

Did you hear about the confused math teacher who didn't believe in addition?

He was feeling rather nonplussed.

What is a math teacher's favorite under-garment?

her algebra

Algebraically Speaking

Why was algebra easier for ancient Romans?

Because X was always ten.

Why are relationships like algebra?

You spend a lot of time thinking about your X and trying to figure out Y?

What do you call a person who uses algebraic equations to calculate coffin sizes?

a mathemortician

My math teacher tried to explain the importance of studying algebra, but I still don't get Y.

If I had a dollar for every time I used algebra in my life, I'd have n dollars.

What does your math teacher have in common with The Beatles?

They both want you to tell them Y.

Why couldn't the angle get a loan?

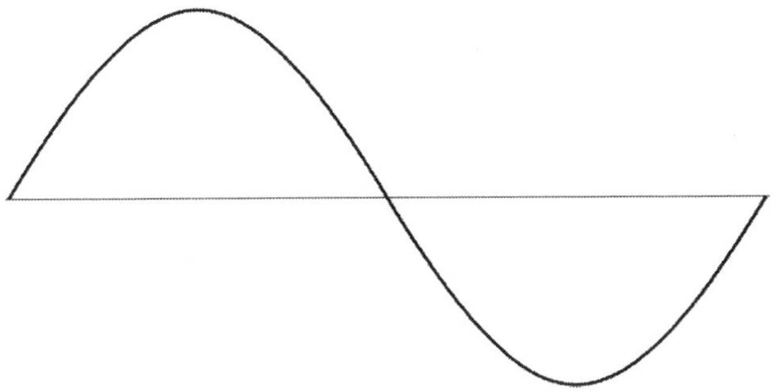

Its parents wouldn't cosine.

A ———————————————————————— **B**

Algebra problem: How do you get from point A to point B?

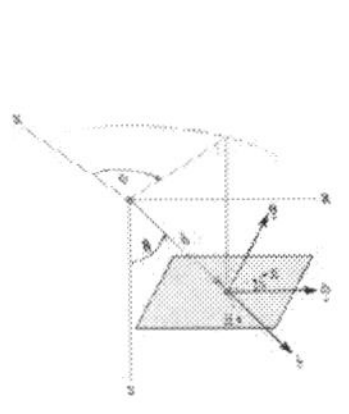

Answer: Take an x-y plane or a rhom-bus.

Math Class

Why did the dime pass math class but the nickel didn't?

Because it had more cents.

Where do math students eat their lunch?

on a times table

Hey math!!

Grow up and solve your own problems.

Social studies is okay, and science isn't too bad…

… but math is the only subject that counts.

Math class was pretty interesting…

…until the teacher started going off on a tangent.

Why were the rabbits in advanced math class?

Because they're so good at multiplying.

What's wrong with the plants in your math class?

They all have square roots.

What do you call a car that has been in a collision with something that has four corners?

a wrecked angle

Did you hear the joke about the statistician?

...probably

We have a German exchange student in our class, but he must not be very good at math.

Every time the teacher asks him if he knows the square root of 81, he says, 'nein.'

Mathematical Menagerie

What did the geometry teacher say when she lost her parrot?

Polygon

What do you get when you cross a dog and a calculator?

a friend you can count on

Why can't snakes multiply?

Because they're adders.

What did the mathematical parrot say?

"Poly wants a cracker…

… and a triangular or square cracker is a polygon."

Why did the chicken cross
the Mobius Strip?

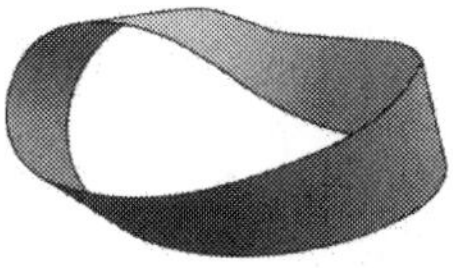

to get to the same side

What school subject do flying insects like
the most?

MOTHematics

What do baby parabolas drink?

quadratic formula

The cowboy brought the cattle into their pen and told the ranch foreman that there were 50 of them. After a moment, the foreman said, “I only count 47.”

The cowboy replied, “That’s because I rounded them up.”

Mathematically Improbable

Normal Dad jokes make me numb.

Math Dad jokes make me number.

Last night I read *War and Peace* in one minute.

According to my calculations, that's three words per minute.

What did zero say to eight?

Nice belt.

Math jokes fall into four categories:

- Algebra jokes are quite formulaic.
- Arithmetic jokes are pretty basic.
- Trigonometry jokes are too graphic.
- Calculus jokes are all derivative.

Can anyone give me an estimate how much I would have to pay for a ball park?

What happens when you put root beer in a square glass?

It just becomes beer.

How did the mathematical magician make 'one' disappear?

He added a 'g' and it was gone.

Why can't a hand be twelve inches long?

Because then it would be a foot.

What do you call a mathematician who spent all summer at the beach?

a tan gent

If you're applying for a job as a statistician, never tell them you're willing to give 110 percent.

Odd Numbers

What do you call a number that can't stay in one place?

a roamin' numeral

My mom would only let me hang out with numbers divisible by 2.

She said all the rest were kind of odd.

Why should you avoid mentioning the number 288?

It's two gross.

My mom asked me to do six odd jobs…

…so I did jobs 1, 3, and 5.

Why was six afraid of seven?

Because seven eight nine.

But why did seven eight nine?

$$3^2 = 9$$

Because you're supposed to eat three squared meals per day.

How do you make seven an even number?

s even

Remove the S.

Seven and three went out on a date.

They were the odd couple.

Whole numbers are half crazy.

Every other one is odd.

To the guy who invented zero…

0

thanks for nothing.

Pi R Funny

My math teacher thinks he's so smart. He keeps talking about pi r squared.

Finally, I had to tell him that pies are round and cakes are square.

Advanced math isn't really that difficult.

In fact, it's as easy as pi.

In math class we had a lesson about pi…

…and it seemed as if it went on forever.

What do you get if you divide the circumference of a jack-o-lantern by its diameter?

a pumpkin pi

"Why don't you get real?" Pi said to the imaginary number.

"Maybe you should be rational," it replied.

What do you get when you divide the circumference of the sun by its diameter?

pi in the sky

Shape Up

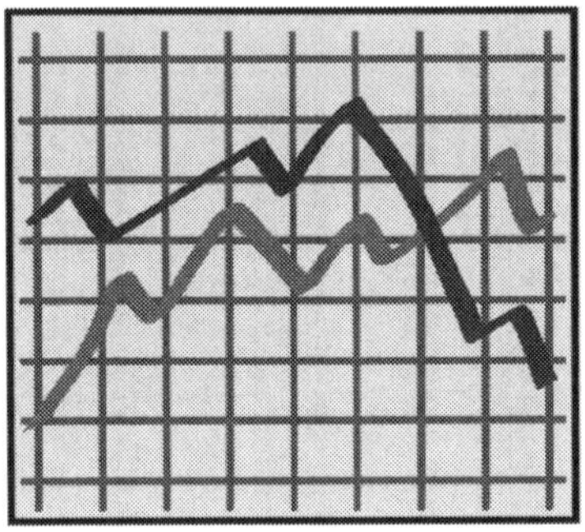

I don't mind doing a little math homework, but graphs are where I have to draw the line.

What did the triangle say to the circle?

Why are circles so hot?

Because they're 360 degrees.

Why are obtuse triangles always so cranky?

Because they're never right.

Have you seen the romance movie about the parallel lines?

SPOILER ALERT:
They never meet.

Did you hear about the circle that stayed in college for his entire life?

Now he has 360 degrees.

What do you call a teakettle whistling on top of a pyramid?

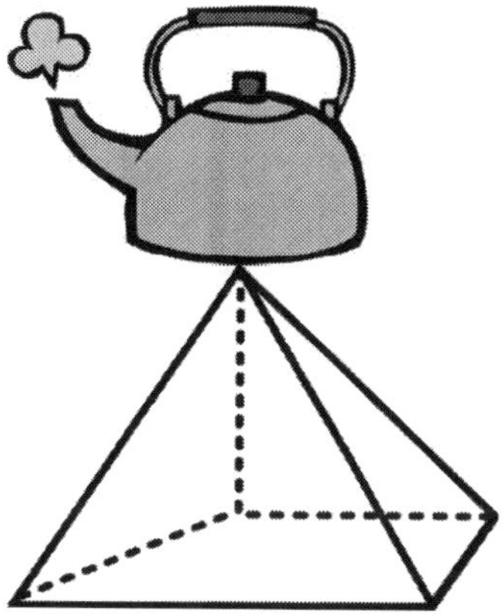

a high-pot-in-use

Why is it good to have triangles on your basketball team?

Because they always make three-pointers.

What geometric shape removes spells and curses?

a hexagon

Why couldn't the geometry teacher play in the staff soccer match?

Because he had twisted his angles.

Sum Funny Jokes

Who says it's okay to count your eggs before they hatch?

the mathemachicken

A butcher is 6 feet tall and wears size 10 shoes.

What does he weigh?

meat

There are only three kinds of people in this world.

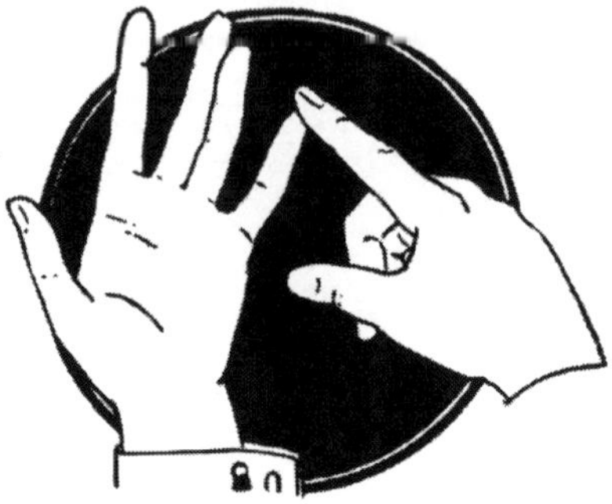

Those who can count, and those who can't.

There were supposed to be a dozen vampires in Transylvania, but I only found 11.

Then I realized that I didn't Count Dracula.

If you get cold, go stand in a corner.

They're usually around 90 degrees.

Not all math jokes stink.

Just sum.

What do you get if you add two apples and three apples?

an easy math problem

Why weren't the 2 fours hungry?

Because they already 8.

Why was the equal sign so humble?

Because she knew she was neither greater than nor less than anyone else.

I had a crazy dream that I weighed less than a thousandth of a gram.

I was like 0mg!!!

Weapons of Math Instruction

Three statisticians are hunting and come upon a deer. The first raises his gun and overshoots. The second aims and undershoots. The third shouts, “We got him!”

Who is the king of the math tools?

the ruler

Beware when math teachers take out their graph paper.

You know they must be plotting something.

What did the math student say to her abacus?

"I can always count on you."

Why was the math book so sad?

Because it had too many problems.

Why don't calculus majors go to bars?

Because you should never drink and derive.

Which is the best
math tool?

multiPLIERS

I stopped watching the new TV series called '100 Divided by 3.'

The plot was tedious, and it had lots of recurring characters.

Why did the school hire an optometrist to teach math class?

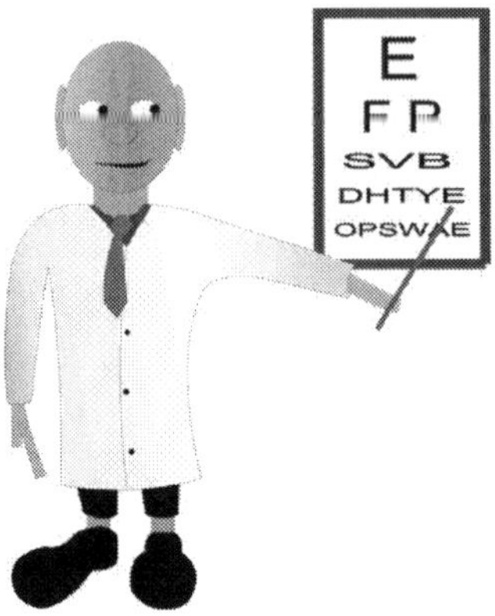

to improve di-vision

Why did the police confiscate the math teacher's compass, protractor and calculators?

Because they were weapons of math instruction.

Dedication

This book is dedicated to Madison Purdy, the greatest math teacher who ever lived. She has all the traits of a perfect teacher. She is passionate about the subject she teaches. She is dedicated to the education of young minds. She has an incredible sense of humor. And she makes learning fun. It is Ralph's most sincere wish that the students of Ms. Purdy realize what a phenomenal teacher they have and that Ms. Purdy realizes what a lasting impact she makes on the next generation. Here's to all the dedicated math teachers of this world. Thanks for all you do!!! Keep teaching, keep learning, and tell a joke every day.